Fact Finders®

GREAT CIVILIZATIONS

# ANCIENT GREECE

## BIRTHPLACE OF DEMOCRACY

by Kim Covert

CAPSTONE PRESS
a capstone imprint

Fact Finders are published by Capstone Press,
151 Good Counsel Drive, P.O. Box 669, Mankato, Minnesota 56002.
www.capstonepub.com

 Books published by Capstone Press are manufactured with paper
containing at least 10 percent post-consumer waste.

*Library of Congress Cataloging-in-Publication Data*
Covert, Kim.
 Ancient Greece : birthplace of democracy / by Kim Covert.
 p. cm.—(Fact finders. Great civilizations)
 Includes bibliographical references and index.
 Summary: "Describes ancient Greece, including its government structure, major achievements and
inventions, and rise to power, as well as its lasting influences on the world"—Provided by publisher.
 ISBN 978-1-4296-6831-6 (library binding)
 ISBN 978-1-4296-7237-5 (paperback)
 1. Greece—History—To 146 B.C.—Juvenile literature. 2. Greece—Civilization—To 146 B.C.—Juvenile
literature. 3. Democracy—Juvenile literature. I. Title.
 DF215.C68 2012
 938—dc22                                                                    2010052223

**Editorial Credits**
Carrie Braulick Sheely and Jennifer Besel, editors; Lori Bye, designer; Svetlana Zhurkin, media
    researcher; Eric Manske, production specialist

**Photo Credits**
Alamy: North Wind Picture Archives, 13, 15; The Bridgeman Art Library: Private Collection/Look and
Learn, 17; Dreamstime: Anthony Baggett, cover and 1 (statue); Getty Images: Stock Montage, 23 (top),
Time Life Pictures/Mansell, 21; The Granger Collection, New York, 5; iStockphoto: Joseph Creech, 23
(bottom), sefaoncul, 11, ZU_09, 7; Shutterstock: Aleksandar Kamasi, 25, Brent Wong, cover (back), 1
(back), Danilo Ascione, cover and 1 (vase), elm, back cover (warrior), Gregor Buir (Greek letters used
as background), Julia Rashid, back cover (background), 28 and 29 (border), Kamira, 18, magicinfoto
(light beige texture paper design), Marilyn Volan (grunge paper design), Petrov Stanislav Eudardovich
(parchment paper design), Rechitan Sorin, cover and 1 (temple), Tim Arbaev, 9, Turkishblue, 10;
Svetlana Zhurkin, 27

Printed in the United States of America in Stevens Point, Wisconsin.
032011        006111WZF11

# TABLE OF CONTENTS

# CHAPTER 1

# AN ANCIENT GREEK TRADITION

The most important sporting event in ancient Greece is underway. Twenty runners get into position on the starting line. A trumpet blares, and sand flies up as the runners blast down the 210-yard (192-meter) track. The crowd cheers as the runners cross the finish line. A wreath of olive leaves is placed on the winner's head.

Later **chariots** line up on an oval track. At the sound of the trumpet, each driver urges his horses forward. In the first turn, a driver cuts in front of another chariot. The two chariots crash into each other and tip over. The horses and drivers crash to the ground. Several more chariots fall in the pileup. The drivers who missed the wreck bolt to the finish line.

**chariot:** a two-wheeled platform used in ancient times that was usually pulled by horses

Chariot racing was one of the crowd's favorite events at the ancient Olympic Games.

**FACT:** Only free men who spoke Greek could compete in chariot racing or other Olympic games.

Footraces and chariot races were just two events of the Olympic Games in ancient Greece. Wrestling, long jump, and boxing were other events. The first recorded Olympics were held in 776 BC. The games took place in Olympia, a town in western Greece. For 1,000 years, the Olympic Games were held every four years.

Today the Olympic Games continue to be held. It is one of many **customs** from ancient Greece. Ancient Greece is often called the cradle of western civilization. It was the birthplace of many modern ideas. These ideas are found in today's governments and **architecture**. Ideas from literature and science also have their roots in ancient Greece.

**custom:** a tradition in culture or society

**architecture:** the style in which buildings are designed

**FACT:** Before each Olympics, the ancient Greeks stopped all warfare. The break in fighting allowed people to travel to and from the games safely.

6

Nearly all of the buildings in the ancient Greek city Olympia were for worshipping gods or for the Olympic Games.

# No Uniforms

Except for the chariot drivers, ancient Olympic athletes didn't wear clothes. Only men competed in the ancient Olympics. Each man protected his skin with olive oil and fine sand. After the games, athletes scraped off the oil and sand using a tool called a strigil.

# CHAPTER 2

# THE FIRST SETTLERS

Early Greek settlers learned the best ways to live in the varied landscape of southern Europe. The Greek mainland bordered the northern Mediterranean Sea. Mountains separated villages. People lived in valleys and on open plains. Only small areas near the coasts were good for farming.

## The Minoans

The Minoans formed the first Greek settlement on the island of Crete south of the mainland. They lived there from 2200 BC to 1450 BC. The Minoans built a huge **port** and a large fleet of ships. Their ships allowed them to trade with other civilizations.

The Minoans also built palaces. They covered the palace walls with paintings showing peaceful, happy people. The Minoans' largest palace honored King Minos. Greeks believed Minos was a son of Zeus. They believed Zeus ruled over all the other gods.

The Minoans built a large palace known as Knossos on Crete. Ruins of the palace still stand.

## The Mycenaeans

By about 1600 BC, the Mycenaeans had settled on the Greek mainland north of Crete. A king ruled each city. Mycenaeans built huge walls around their palaces. Paintings, gold, and jewels decorated the palaces.

**port:** a harbor or place where boats and ships can dock safely

The Mycenaeans were great warriors. Around 1450 BC, they invaded Crete and conquered the Minoans. According to legend, around 1220 BC the Mycenaeans also conquered Troy. This city was on the northwestern coast of Asia Minor. Today the area includes the country of Turkey.

Few Mycenaeans remained in Crete or the Greek mainland by 1200 BC. Their palaces on the mainland were destroyed. Historians believe they were invaded by another civilization. The Dorians from northern Greece later took over Crete.

The ruins of Troy were discovered in the 1800s. Before the discovery, some people believed the city never existed.

re-creation of the Trojan horse

# Were the Trojans Tricked?

Stories about the Trojan War were passed down through time. One of most famous involves a huge wooden horse. For many years, tall walls around Troy kept the Greeks from invading. To sneak in, the Greeks gave a hollow wooden horse to the Trojans as a gift. The Trojans dragged the horse into the city. They didn't know Greek soldiers were hiding inside. At night, the soldiers climbed out and opened Troy's gates. The Greek army then entered the city and defeated the Trojans.

## The Dark Age

Historians know little about Greece from 1100 to 800 BC. During this time, Greece was a land of small farming villages. These villages had little contact with one another. Historians call this period the Dark Age.

Around 800 BC, the Greeks appeared in history again. They built **colonies** in Europe and Africa. They traded with people in western Asia and learned to make iron tools.

The Phoenicians lived across the Mediterranean Sea to the east. The Greeks traded with the Phoenicians and learned their alphabet and writing system. They also learned about Phoenician art and shipbuilding. These new skills helped end Greece's Dark Age.

**colony:** a place that is settled by people from another country and is controlled by that country

Ancient ports along the Mediterranean Sea were busy, crowded places as people received and sent out goods.

**FACT:** Historians have not found any Greek writings from the Dark Age. They believe the Greeks had no system of reading or writing during this time.

# CHAPTER 3

# RISE TO POWER

By the end of the Dark Age, the Greeks had built many villages. Most villages were built around a high hilltop called an acropolis. The farms and villages surrounding each acropolis joined to form a city-state. Each city-state ruled itself and had its own army.

By 700 BC, hundreds of independent city-states had formed. The two most powerful were Athens and Sparta.

## Athens

Athens was on the east side of Greece near the Aegean Sea. Athens had a port city called Piraeus. This port allowed Athens to launch its powerful navy and trade ships. Long walls joined Athens and Piraeus.

Athenians welcomed new ideas and customs. They believed that a city-state should serve all of its citizens. Their beliefs led them to create a **democracy**.

Athenians built large temples on top of a high hilltop called the acropolis (seen at top left).

In the democracy, each free male citizen in Athens could vote on laws and choose leaders. Women and slaves could not vote. An assembly made governmental decisions.

**democracy:** a kind of government in which citizens vote for their leaders

## Sparta

Sparta was about 150 miles (240 km) southwest of Athens. Mountains around Sparta protected the city-state. Spartans were different from Athenians. Spartans wanted no contact with outsiders, and they were against change.

Sparta and Athens also had different governments. Two kings and a council of elders ruled Sparta. Only rich people served on the council.

Sparta's society was based on the military. Every adult male was a full-time soldier. Soldiers were not allowed to work other jobs.

## The Persian Wars

Persia was a large empire east of Greece that covered much of Asia. King Darius I of Persia wanted to rule Greece.

In 490 BC, Darius' army landed at the village of Marathon north of Athens. An army of 10,000 Athenians marched to Marathon to face the 60,000 Persians. Athens won the battle in a surprise victory.

Athenian soldiers gained victory at the Battle of Marathon by charging and surrounding the Persian soldiers.

Ten years later, Darius' son Xerxes returned to Greece. He brought an army of 200,000 men. Athens and Sparta led a united army of all Greek city-states. After a year of fighting, the Greeks defeated the Persians in 479 BC. Their victory kept the Persians from taking over Europe.

**FACT:** The Greeks used a phalanx formation to defeat the Persians. They lined up side by side and several rows deep. Each man used his shield to protect the soldier next to him.

## The Golden Age of Athens

After the Persian Wars, Athens entered its Golden Age. During this period, Athens' power reached its peak. The Greeks made great advances in art, science, and government.

Pericles was the leader of Athens from 461 to 429 BC. He supported democracy. He also started a system of payment for government service. The earlier system did not pay government workers. Only rich people could afford to serve in the government. The new system allowed anyone to earn a living by working in government.

Pericles planned to make Athens a model for other city-states. He helped build a strong navy. Athens became wealthy through trade with other lands. Athens was also a model for the arts. The government supported the work of architects, artists, and writers.

a sculpture of Pericles

# Ancient Greece, 500 BC–336 BC

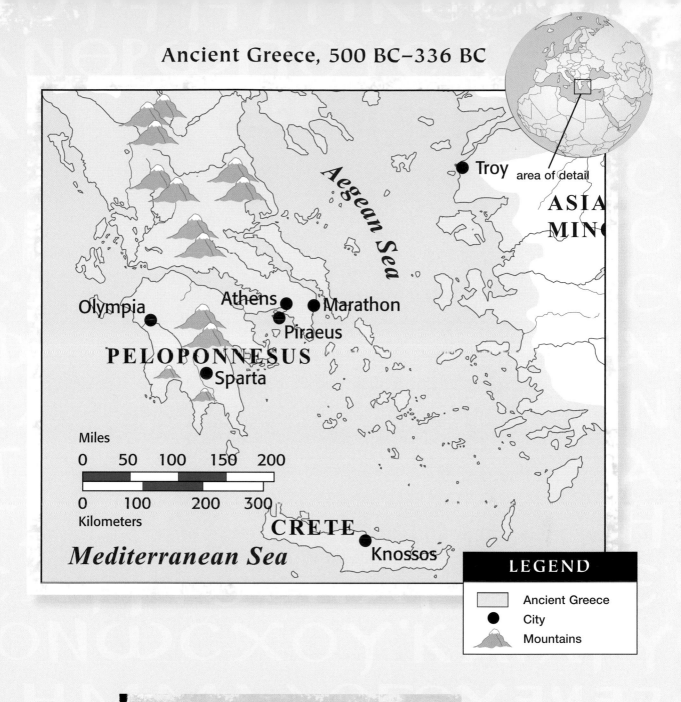

Troy

area of detail

ASIA MINO

Aegean Sea

Olympia

Athens

Marathon

Piraeus

PELOPONNESUS

Sparta

Miles

0    50    100    150    200

0    100    200    300

Kilometers

CRETE

Mediterranean Sea

Knossos

LEGEND

Ancient Greece

City

Mountains

**FACT:** Pericles' name in Greek means "surrounded by glory."

# CHAPTER 4

# DECLINE of GREECE

The Persian Wars led the Greek city-states to make changes. Many city-states joined together and agreed to protect each other. This **alliance** was known as the Delian League. Delian League members gave ships and money to the league. They kept the money in the league treasury.

Athens' government made decisions for the league. Athenians began taking the league's money to build temples and new colonies. The city-state built a large and powerful empire in the Mediterranean region.

## The Peloponnesian War

Over time, Athens' power caused problems. Sparta and Athens became enemies. Sparta was afraid that Athens' power would reach too far. Other Greek city-states were upset that Athens was taking money from the Delian League.

**alliance:** an agreement between groups to work together

A major sea battle of the Peloponnesian War happened in the harbor of Syracuse. Athens' navy was defeated there.

In 431 BC, Sparta declared war on Athens. For 27 years, Athens and Sparta fought in the Peloponnesian War. Allies of each city-state joined in the fighting. Sparta's armies won many land battles. Athens' navy won many sea battles. With help from Persia, Sparta forced Athens to surrender in 404 BC.

After the Peloponnesian War, other city-states fought one another. The fighting lasted for more than 30 years.

# The Hellenistic Age

In 359 BC, Philip II became king of Macedonia. Many small warlike tribes lived in this area north of Greece. Philip II built a strong army with the tribesmen. He then attacked Greece, which had been weakened by years of fighting. In 338 BC, Philip II defeated the Greeks.

In 336 BC, Philip II's son Alexander became king. A strong military leader, he became known as Alexander the Great. His army conquered Persia, Egypt, and many other lands.

After Alexander's death in 323 BC, Greece entered the Hellenistic Age. Alexander's generals fought to control his empire. They divided Greece into the Ptolemaic, Seleucid, and Macedonian kingdoms. The power of the city-states faded. But the new rulers helped spread the Greek way of life.

Greek traditions spread from what is now southern France to present-day northern Afghanistan. A huge library was built in Alexandria, Egypt. The Greeks developed new forms of literature and sculpture. The study of **philosophy** also became widespread during the Hellenistic Age.

# A Love for Greek Culture

Philosopher Aristotle was one of Alexander the Great's childhood teachers. Aristotle taught Alexander to respect the Greek way of life. Years later, Alexander founded many military colonies in the lands he conquered. The Greek language was spoken in Alexander's colonies. The colonists copied Greek architecture, law, and art. They studied Greek science and philosophy. By spreading Greek culture, Alexander helped it continue after his death.

Alexander the Great (right) listens to his teacher Aristotle (left).

an ancient Greek tablet

philosophy: the study of truth, knowledge, and ideas

# CHAPTER 5

# LASTING ACHIEVEMENTS

Around 275 BC, the Romans defeated King Pyrrhus in Italy. Rome gradually took over other kingdoms. By 31 BC, Rome had defeated the last Greek kingdom. This defeat brought an end to the Hellenistic Age and, soon afterward, ancient Greece.

Today the ideas of ancient Greece still influence the modern world. The ancient Greeks made lasting contributions to government, architecture, science, and medicine. They also developed **drama**, literature, and philosophy.

## Government

Democracy is now a common form of government. Ancient Greeks also developed political speeches and debates, which are both still practiced.

drama: an art form that includes plays

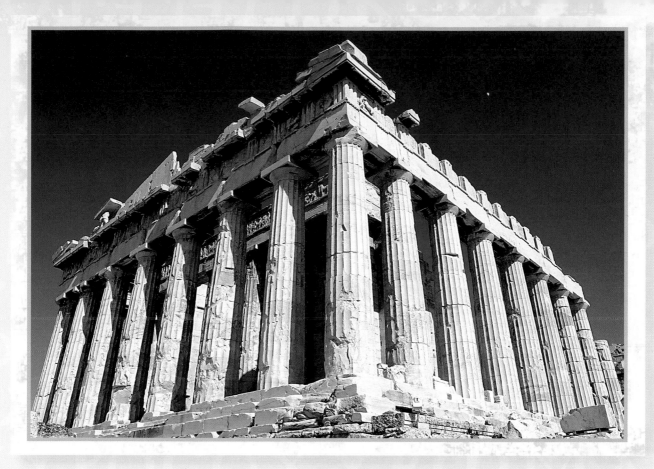

Like many other ancient Greek temples, the Parthenon is rectangular with columns holding up the roof.

## Architecture

The most famous example of Greek architecture is the Parthenon. Completed in 432 BC, this temple honored the goddess Athena.

Modern architects base many of their designs on Greek styles. Court buildings, capitol buildings, and presidential homes have all used Greek architecture.

**FACT:** Athena was the goddess of war and wisdom.

## Science and Philosophy

Many great philosophers and scientists lived in ancient Greece. Scientists such as Ptolemy and Archimedes made important discoveries, including how levers work. The ideas of philosophers Aristotle, Plato, and Socrates are still discussed today.

Hippocrates was an ancient Greek doctor. He is often called the father of medicine. He developed a promise to heal the sick called the Hippocratic oath. Today many medical students take this oath when they become doctors.

## Sports

Ancient Greeks believed in achieving a balance between work and play. They felt that a good education should promote both strong minds and bodies. The modern Olympics show Greece's sporting influence today. The Olympics are now held every two years. Many cities around the world have hosted the Olympics.

**FACT:** Athens hosted the first modern Olympic Games in 1896. Athletes from 14 countries competed.

In Aesop's fable "The Fox and the Grapes," the fox is unable to get grapes from a tree. The fable shows people that it's easy to say that things they can't have aren't worth having anyway.

## Drama and Writing

When you go to a play, you are seeing an art form created by the ancient Greeks. Even **fables** have their roots in ancient Greece. In the 500s BC, Aesop wrote hundreds of fables, including the classic "The Fox and the Grapes." Many of Aesop's fables are still told today.

From finely crafted buildings to timeless stories, ancient Greek culture is easy to find in everyday life. The next time you attend a play or wrestling match, think of how this great ancient culture helped shape the world.

**fable:** a story that teaches a lesson

# TIMELINE

**2200–1450 BC**

Crete is home to the Minoan civilization.

**1600–1200 BC**

The Mycenaeans live on the Greek mainland.

**776 BC**

Greeks hold the first known Olympic Games.

**479 BC**

Greek city-states unite to defeat the Persian army.

1000            700            500

**1220 BC**

According to legend, the Mycenaeans conquer Troy.

**1100–800 BC**

Greece does not appear in historical records; this period is known as the Dark Age of Greece.

**490 BC**

The Greeks defeat the Persians at Marathon.

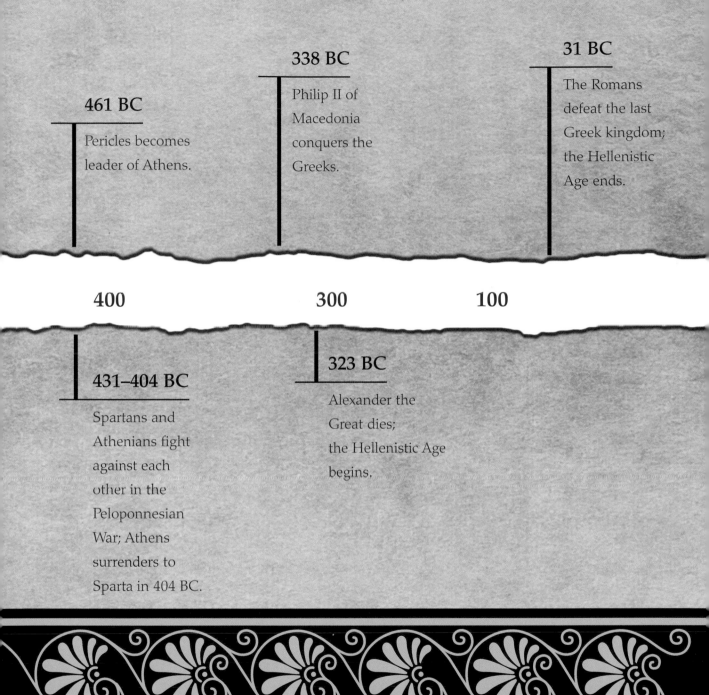

**461 BC**

Pericles becomes leader of Athens.

**338 BC**

Philip II of Macedonia conquers the Greeks.

**31 BC**

The Romans defeat the last Greek kingdom; the Hellenistic Age ends.

400

300

100

**431–404 BC**

Spartans and Athenians fight against each other in the Peloponnesian War; Athens surrenders to Sparta in 404 BC.

**323 BC**

Alexander the Great dies; the Hellenistic Age begins.

# GLOSSARY

**alliance** (uh-LY-uhnts)—an agreement between groups to work together

**architecture** (AR-kuh-tek-chuhr)—the style in which buildings are designed

**chariot** (CHAYR-ee-uht)—a two-wheeled fighting platform used in ancient times that was usually pulled by horses

**colony** (KAH-luh-nee)—a place that is settled by people from another country and is controlled by that country

**custom** (KUHS-tuhm)—a tradition in a culture or society

**democracy** (de-MOK-ruh-see)—a kind of government in which citizens vote for their leaders

**drama** (DRAH-muh)—an art form that includes plays

**fable** (FAY-buhl)—a story that teaches a lesson

**philosophy** (fuh-LOSS-uh-fee)—the study of truth, knowledge, and ideas

**port** (PORT)—a harbor or place where boats and ships can dock safely

# READ MORE

**Callery, Sean.** *The Dark History of Ancient Greece.* Dark Histories. New York: Marshall Cavendish Benchmark, 2010.

**Green, Jen.** *Hail! Ancient Greeks.* Hail! History. New York: Crabtree Pub., 2011.

**Malam, John.** *How the Ancient Greeks Lived.* Life in Ancient Times. New York: Gareth Stevens, 2011.

# INTERNET SITES

FactHound offers a safe, fun way to find Internet sites related to this book. All of the sites on FactHound have been researched by our staff.

Here's all you do:

Visit *www.facthound.com*

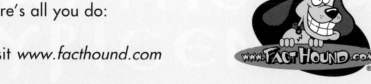

Type in this code: 9781429668316

Check out projects, games and lots more at
**www.capstonekids.com**

# INDEX